BY JUNE WOODMAN

ILLUSTRATED BY PAMELA STOREY

GONDOLA

It is a very wet day.
The rain is coming down very hard. Flippy Frog comes hopping along down the lane.
Plop! Plop! Plop!
"I like wet days," says Flippy Frog. "It is never too wet for me."

Flippy comes to Cuddly Cat's little house.
He hops up to the window.
Plop! Plop! Plop!
When he looks inside, Flippy sees a nurse.
She has a white cap with a red cross on it. She has a long white skirt.
"Where is Cuddly?" says Flippy Frog.
He hops away very fast.

Soon Flippy comes to Hoppy Rabbit's house. Hoppy is busy mending his gate.

"Help!" says Flippy. "There is a nurse at Cuddly's house."

"Where is Cuddly?" says Hoppy.

"She must be sick," says Flippy. "We must help her."

So they hurry back to Cuddly Cat's house.

They both look in at
Cuddly Cat's window.
"I see a nurse with a red
cross on her cap," says
Hoppy.
"I told you so," says
Flippy.
But where is Cuddly Cat?
"Stay here, Flippy," says
Hoppy. "Cuddly must be sick.
I will tell Paddy Dog."
He hops away down the lane
as fast as he can.

Paddy Dog is in his house. He is mending his clock. "There is a nurse in poor Cuddly's house," says Hoppy.
"She must be sick," says Paddy Dog. "We must go and help her."
They both hurry back and look in at the window.

"I can see the nurse," says Paddy Dog.
"I told you so," says Hoppy.
But Paddy can see someone else.
"Look! I can see a doctor too," he says.
"Oh, POOR Cuddly!" says Hoppy. "She MUST be sick."
But where is Cuddly Cat?

"Stay here," says Paddy.
"I will go and tell Bossy Bear."
He runs as fast as he can to Bossy's house. Bossy is mending his window.
"Cuddly Cat must be sick. We can see a nurse and a doctor in her house," says Paddy Dog.
"Poor Cuddly," says Bossy. "We must go and help her."

They run back and look into Cuddly Cat's window.
"I can see the nurse and the doctor," says Paddy Dog.
But Bossy Bear can see someone else.
"Help!" he says. "I can see a pirate there too.
The pirate has a black hat and big black boots."

"What can we do?" says Paddy Dog.
"You stay here," says Bossy. "I will go and tell Merry Mole."
He runs off as fast as he can and soon he sees Merry Mole. Merry is busy digging a hole.
"Help!" says Bossy. "There is a nurse in Cuddly Cat's house. There is a doctor there and a pirate too."

They run back to the house.
They look in at the window.
"Poor Cuddly!" says Merry.
"I can see the nurse and
the doctor and the pirate."
"I told you so," says Bossy.
"And there is someone else.
I can see a funny clown,"
says Merry Mole.
But where is Cuddly Cat?

"What can we do?" says Bossy Bear.
"You stay here," says Merry. "I will go and tell Dilly Duck."
He runs as fast as he can. Dilly is coming down the lane. Her three little ducklings are with her.
"Help!" says Merry Mole. "There is a nurse, a doctor, a pirate and a clown. They are all in Cuddly Cat's house!"

"You are silly!" says Dilly.
"Come and see," says
Merry Mole.
So they all hurry to the house.
The three little ducklings
run to look in.
"We can see a nurse and
a doctor, a pirate and
a clown," they say.
"I told you so," says Merry.
"Look! There is a king too,"
say the little ducklings.
But . . .
WHERE IS CUDDLY CAT?

Then Dilly Duck looks in. "You ARE silly!" says Dilly. "Here is Cuddly Cat. Here are Flippy, Hoppy, Paddy and Bossy too. They are all playing with Cuddly's dressing-up box."

"Come in," says Cuddly Cat, the nurse. "We can all play dressing-up. It is a lovely game for a wet day!"

Say these words again

plop
house
white
cross
black
pirate
stay

someone
mending
skirt
hurry
sick
doctor
poor